EXPLORE THE DEEP BLUE SEA TO LEARN YOUR ABCS

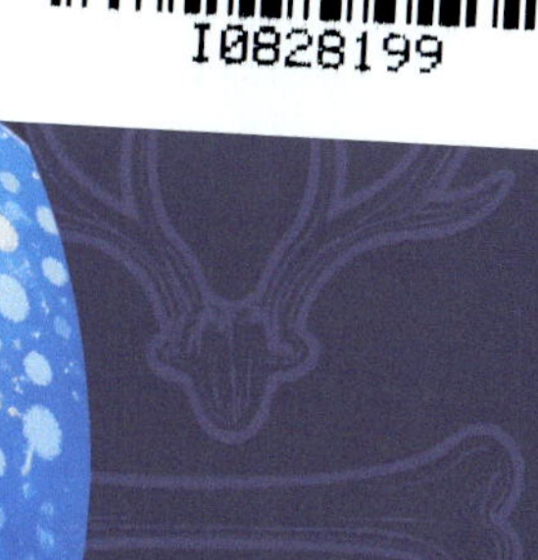

B IS FOR BLUE WHALE

ANTLER & BONE

ISBN: 978-1-966417-48-4 (PRINT)

PUBLISHED BY ANTLER & BONE. ANTLER & BONE'S TITLES MAY BE PURCHASED IN BULK FOR EDUCATIONAL, BUSINESS, FUNDRAISING, OR SALES PROMOTIONAL USE. FOR INFORMATION, PLEASE EMAIL HELLO@ANTLERANDBONE.COM

FIRST PRINT EDITION: 2026

ANTLER & BONE
WWW.ANTLERANDBONE.COM

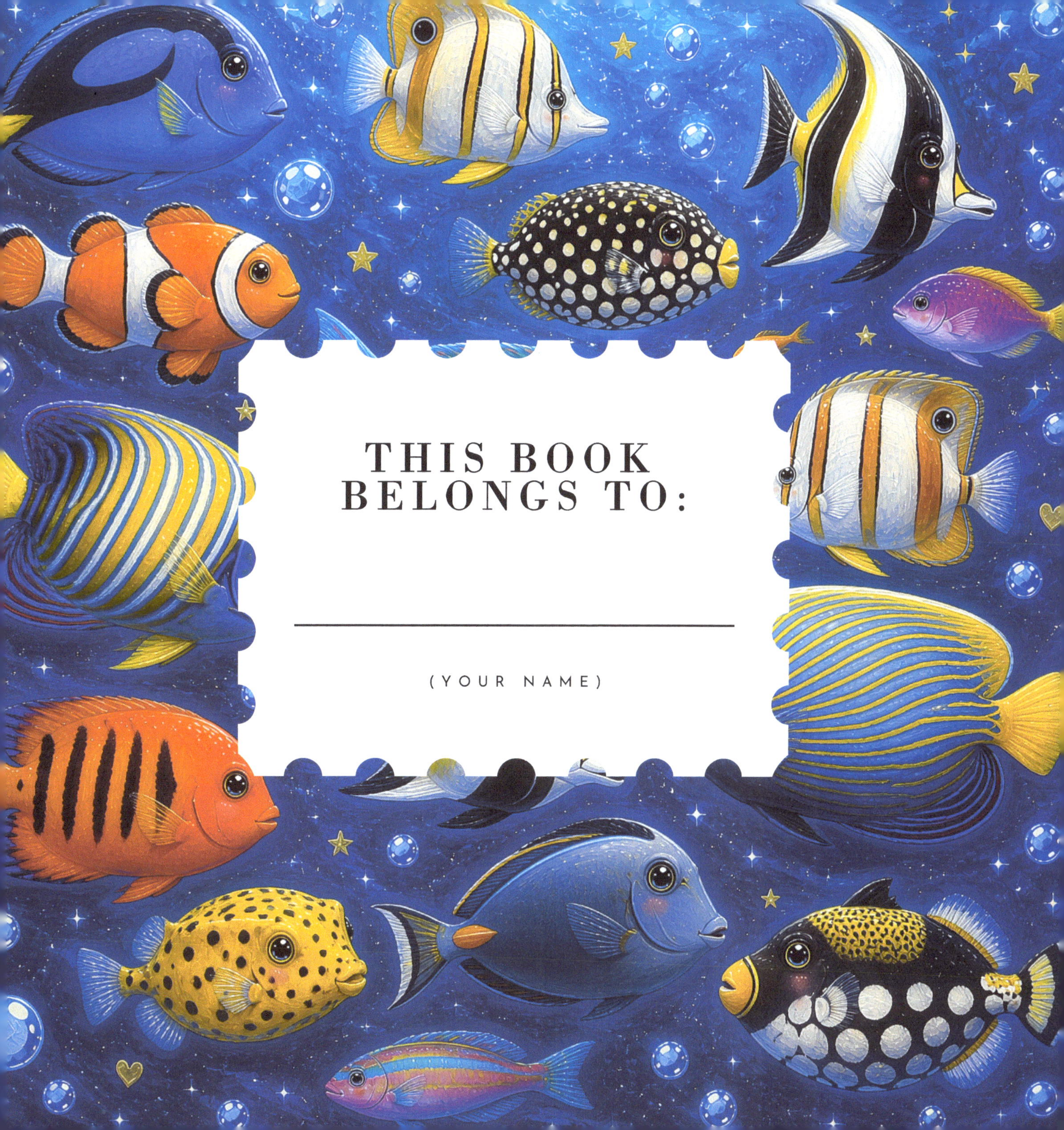
THIS BOOK
BELONGS TO:
(YOUR NAME)

Aa

ANGELFISH

Angelfish have tall, pretty fins that look like soft wings in the water. They glide slow, like they are dancing in the sea.

Bb

BLUE WHALE

The blue whale is the biggest animal in the whole world. Its heart is as big as a small car and beats like a deep drum.

Cc
CLOWNFISH
Clownfish live in soft, wiggly sea homes called anemones. They are not afraid, even when the anemone stings others.

Dd
DOLPHIN
Dolphins are very smart and love to play and jump in the waves. they talk to each other with happy clicks and whistles.

Ee

EEL

Eels have long, wiggly bodies like swimming ribbons. They like to hide in rocks and peek out with curious eyes.

Ff

FLOUNDER

Flounder are flat fish that lie on the sandy sea floor. Both of their eyes sit on one side of their head!

Gg

GROUPER

Groupers have big mouths that can gulp food in one quick bite. Some can even change color like a magic trick.

Hh

HAMMERHEAD SHARK

Hammerhead sharks have wide, funny-shaped heads like a hammer. Their eyes sit far apart so they can see all around.

Ii
ICEFISH
Icefish live in very cold water near ice and snow. Their blood is clear, not red like ours.

Jj

JELLYFISH

Jellyfish have soft, wobbly bodies that float like blobs of slime. They drift with the water and glow in the dark sea.

Kk
KRILL
Krill are tiny sea creatures that swim in big, busy groups. Even giant whales love to eat these little snacks.

Ll
LOBSTER
Lobsters have strong claws to grab and hold their food. They can even grow new claws if they lose one.

Mm

MANATEE

Manatees are slow, gentle swimmers who love to munch on sea grass. They are often called sea cows.

Nn

NARWHAL

Narwhals have a long, twisty tusk that looks like a unicorn horn. It grows right out of their head!

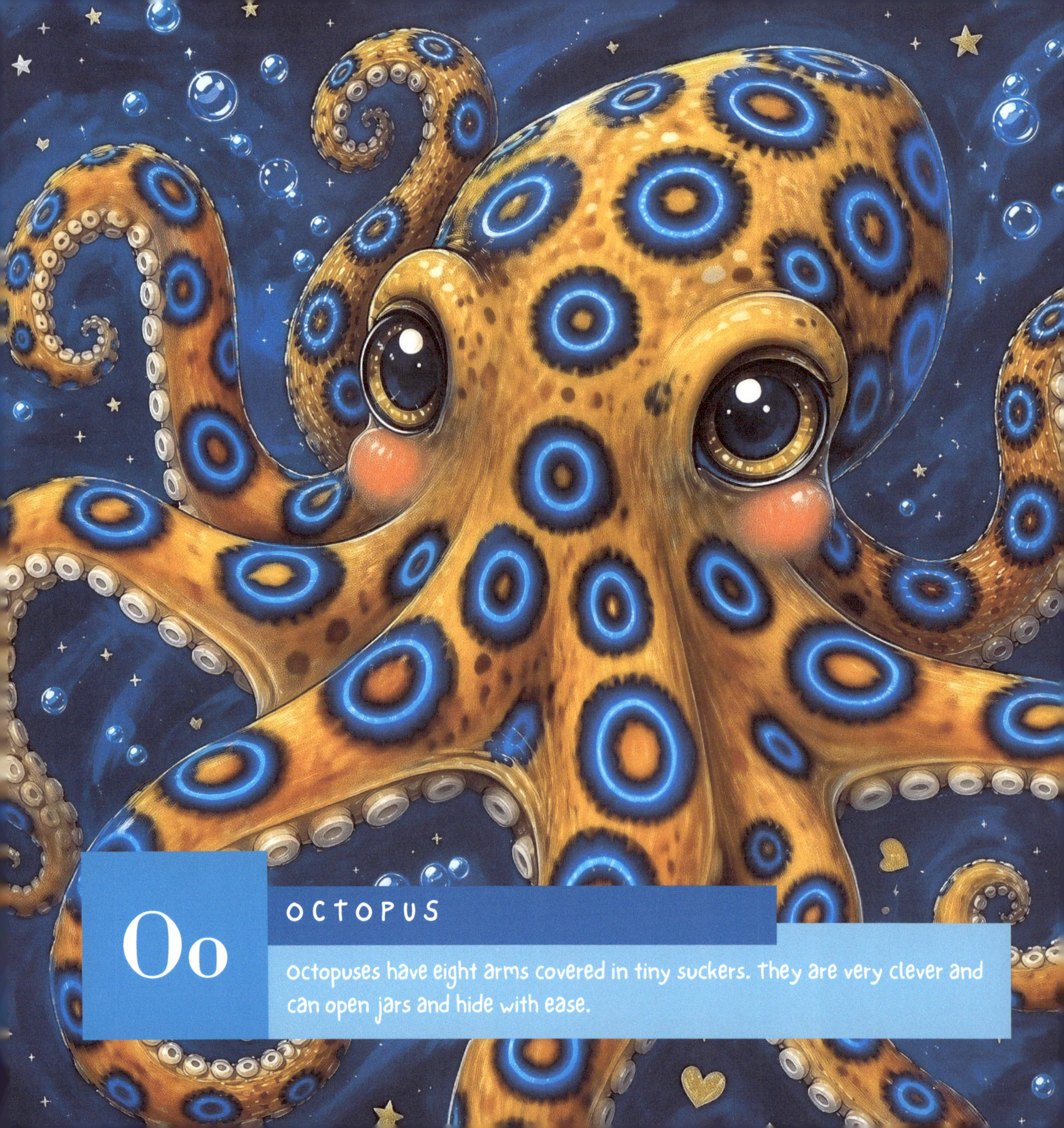

Oo

OCTOPUS

Octopuses have eight arms covered in tiny suckers. They are very clever and can open jars and hide with ease.

Pp
PUFFERFISH
Pufferfish can puff up into a big, round ball when they feel scared. This makes it hard for others to eat them.

Qq

QUEEN ANGELFISH

Queen angelfish help keep coral reefs clean by eating sponges. This helps the reef stay healthy and grow strong.

Rr

RAY (MANTA RAY)

Rays glide through the water like flying carpets. They flap their wide fins as they move along the ocean floor.

Ss
SEAHORSE
Seahorses swim upright, like tiny horses in the sea. The daddy seahorse carries the babies!

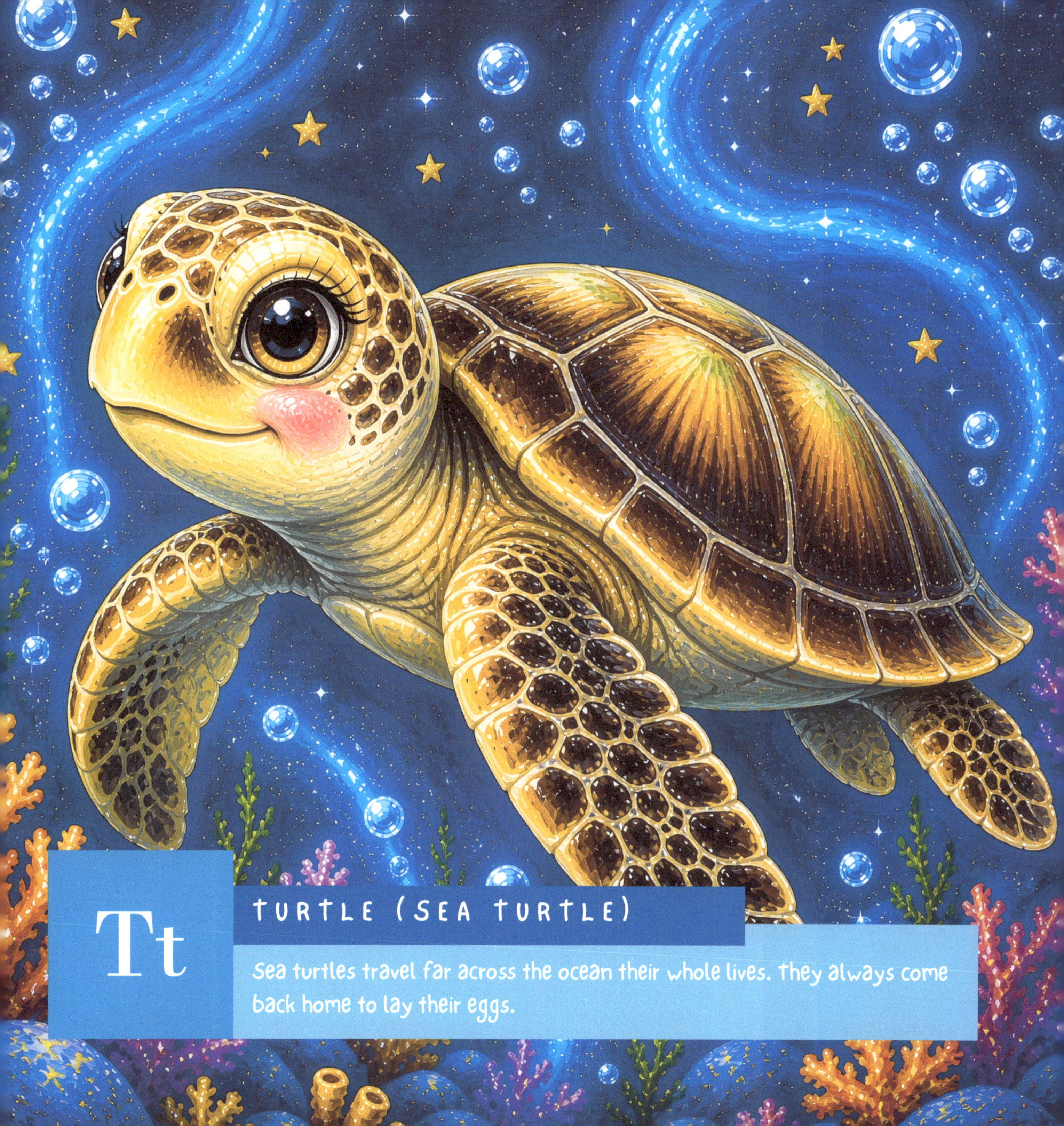

Tt

TURTLE (SEA TURTLE)

Sea turtles travel far across the ocean their whole lives. They always come back home to lay their eggs.

Uu
URCHIN (SEA URCHIN)
Sea urchins are round and covered in pointy spines. These pincushion shaped creatures walk along the sea floor.

Vv

VAMPIRE SQUID

The vampire squid has a dark, cape-like body that spreads like a cloak. It glows softly in the deep, dark sea.

Ww

WALRUS

Walruses have long tusks and big whiskers on their face. They use their tusks to pull themselves onto ice.

Xx
X-RAY FISH
X-ray fish have see-through bodies you can peek inside. You can even see their tiny bones!

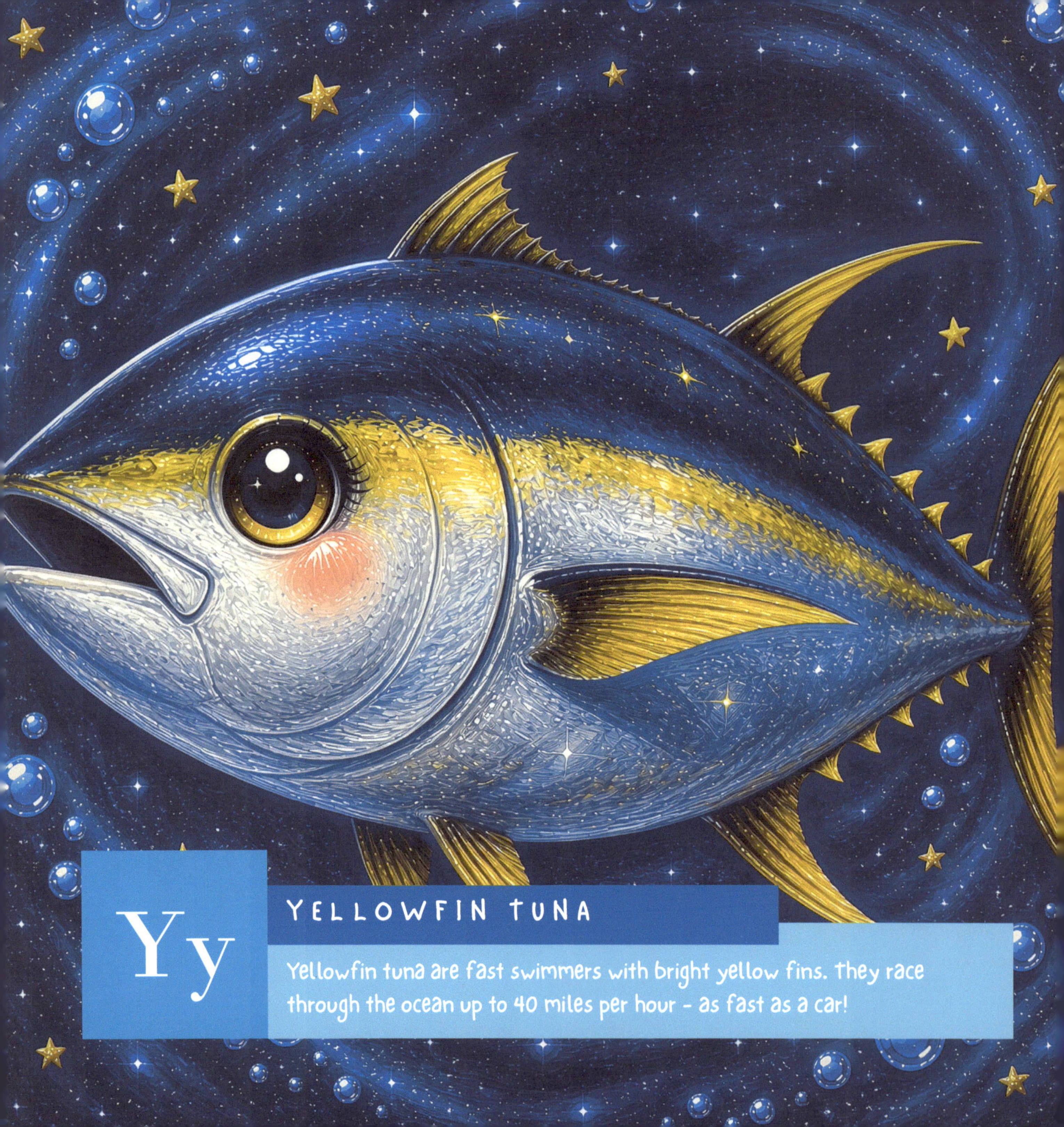
Yy
YELLOWFIN TUNA
Yellowfin tuna are fast swimmers with bright yellow fins. they race through the ocean up to 40 miles per hour - as fast as a car!

Zz
ZOOPLANKTON
Zooplankton are tiny sea drifters you can barely see. Many sea animals eat them to grow big and strong.

EVERY MONTH WE ARE CHOOSING A LUCKY READER TO WIN A FREE BOOK.
JUST CREATE AN ACCOUNT AT THE LINK BELOW TO ENTER FOR A CHANCE TO WIN.

ANTLERANDBONE.COM/FREE

www.ingramcontent.com/pod-product-compliance
Lightning Source LLC
LaVergne TN
LVHW070203110826
845147LV00002B/483

* 9 7 8 1 9 6 6 4 1 7 4 8 4 *